Wet Tropics
Destinations
World Heritage Area

Mike Prociv

Dedication

I dedicate this book to all those natural history photographers whose images generated appreciation, awe and passion about the wet tropics area. These images fed a groundswell of public opinion, that culminated in the Australian Government protecting the area in perpetuity. The role of the photographer's work in conservation is often an understated one.

Published by Mike Prociv Books

PO Box 26 Smithfield Qld 4878 Australia

Phone (07) 4057 7935 Fax (07) 4057 5070

Photography and text by Mike Prociv
Wetro-pics Photographic Library

Graphic Design by Paul Nockolds

© Michael Prociv

Destinations of the Wet Tropics World Heritage Area

ISBN 0-9758055-0-9
Printed in China

All rights reserved. No part of this publication may be reproduced, stored in a retrieval system or transmitted in any form or by any means, electronic, mechanical, photocopying, recording, or otherwise, without prior permission from the publisher.

About this book

40 of the most popular and easier to access destinations have been presented here. This depiction is a simple representation to show what each site has to offer. For further information about walking tracks, camping grounds, permits and facilities, please contact the Queensland Parks and Wildlife Service information centres at Townsville, Cardwell, Cairns, Atherton or Mossman.

For simplicity, the Wet Tropics World Heritage Area is divided into four districts that make logical travel routes. The destinations are listed as the majority of visitors to the region travel: using Cairns as a starting point. Some popular regional recreation sites that are not shown here may be outside the Wet Tropics World Heritage Area.

Contents

Introduction
The Wet Tropics World Heritage Area 1
The World's Oldest Surviving Rainforest 2
Naming the Wet Tropics 3
Presenting the WTWHA 4
Destinations in the Wet tropics World Heritge Area 5

Northern Destinations
Captain Cook Highway – Oak Beach to Buchan Point 10
Mossman Gorge 11
Alexandra Range Lookout 13
Jindalba 14
Maardja Botanical Walk 15
Myall Beach-Dubuji 16
Cape Tribulation 17
Black Mountain 18

Tablelands Destinations
Barron Falls 22
Bunda Dibandji (Bare Hill) 24
Lake Barrine 25
Lake Eacham 26
Cathedral Fig 27
Curtain Fig 28
Mount Bartle Frere 29
The Crater 30

Central Coast Destinations
Crystal Cascades 34
Lake Morris 35
Walshs Pyramid 36
Babinda Boulders 37
Etty Bay 38
North Bramston Beach 39
Josephine Falls 40
Goldsborough Valley 41
Tchupala Falls 42
Nandroya Falls 43
Misty Mountains 44
Bicton Hill 45
Lacey Creek - Licuala 46

Southern Destinations
Tully River 50
Murray Falls 51
Jourama Falls 52
Wet Tropics Great Walk 53
Broadwater 55
Wallaman Falls 56
Paluma 57

About The Author 59

Upland rainforest, Mossman Gorge.

Introduction

Eastern escarpment of Mount Bellenden Ker

The Wet Tropics World Heritage Area

Much of the Wet Tropics region was proclaimed State Forest and Timber Reserve in the 1930's, primarily as a resource for logging timber and as catchments for water supply. The area supplied most of Australia's demand for native softwood and cabinet timbers, accounting for about 70% of Queensland export earnings. Some small areas were set aside as national parks as they were considered to have high scenic value.

Clearing of tropical lowland rainforest at Tully.

Against the wishes of the Queensland Government, in 1988 the Australian Government successfully lodged an application to the World Heritage Convention for the wet tropical rainforests to be inscribed on the World Heritage List. At that time, a little over two thirds of the Wet Tropics World Heritage Area (WTWHA) was state forest, with the remainder being national park and some freehold private property.

The Australian Government ruled that logging within the WTWHA would not be permitted, effectively shutting down the timber industry.

To achieve World Heritage listing, the area had to fulfil at least one of the following criteria:

- *Represent a major stage of the Earth's evolutionary history; or*
- *Provide outstanding examples of ongoing geological and biological processes; or*
- *Contain superlative natural phenomena or areas of natural beauty; or*
- *Contain the most important natural habitats for the conservation of biological diversity.*

In fact the WTWHA fulfils all of the above criteria.

It took the Queensland Government another 16 years to transfer the State Forest and Timber Reserve tenures to effectively make 95% of the WTWHA national park.

"The primary goal of the Wet Tropics World Heritage Area is to implement Australia's international duty to protect, present, rehabilitate and transmit to future generations the Wet Tropics World Heritage Area, within the meaning of the World Heritage Convention".

The World's Oldest Surviving Rainforest

The rainforests within the WTWHA are believed to be the world's oldest. They have been growing continuously for the past 100 million years.

Individual trees of the species *Xanthophyllum octandrum* (McIntyre's Boxwood) are estimated to be in excess of 3,500 years old. Rare Stockwellia trees, still living in a few isolated patches, appear to be the ancestral stock from which today's eucalypts evolved. Numbering only in the hundreds, some individuals have stems up to 2.5 metres in diameter with buttresses 12 metres across and 5 metres high. Most are hollowed out, make accurate dating impossible, however these must be very old trees.

Individual *Lepidozamia hopei* found growing today along the coastal lowlands around Tully stand up to twelve metres tall. These cycads grow at a rate of one centremetre per year, making some of these plants 1200 years old. The seed bearing female trees have scars where Aborigines cut footholds using stone axes, enabling them to climb straight trunks to harvest this staple food. The one tree would have been climbed to feed at least sixty generations of people.

Trunk of Lepidozamia hopei with visible foot-hold scars.

Above: Barron Falls in flood.

Right: Upland rainforest stream in Mossman Gorge.

Naming the Wet Tropics

The Wet Tropics World Heritage Area lies along a 400 kilometre section of coastal ranges between Townsville and Cooktown in north Queensland. The area is a discontinuous strip of 9,200 square kilometres, incorporating small sections of rugged coastline, steep escarpment slopes and upland plateau with deeply gouged gorges. The equivalent area would make a square 96km x 96km. This represents about 0.1% of the surface area of the Australian continent.

The Wet Tropics World Heritage Area derives its name from the high seasonal rainfall, which averages between 1200mm in the drier sections, to 5000mm in the wetter. During one cyclonic year, the summit weather station on Mount Bellenden Ker measured a record annual rainfall in excess of 13 metres.

The towns of Tully and Babinda, which compete for the annual "Golden Gumboot" Award for being Australia's wettest town, receive an average 5000mm of rainfall per year.

Right: Rafting on the North Johnston River.

View from a Skyrail gondola of the Kuranda Range.

Presenting the WTWHA

One of the five primary goals of managing the WTWHA is to:

Present the heritage values of the WHA to local, national and international communities in a way that creates the greatest understanding of, and support for, this unique area.

At the time of listing, there were about 300,000 people living within and adjacent to the WTWHA. Annually the area receives around one million visits by local, domestic and international tourists. Each year the rate of international tourism growth has averaged seven per cent. Tourism to the WTWHA is second only to Great Barrier Reef tourism and, when combined, is the region's largest industry.

Picnic area at Lake Eacham.

The Wet Tropics World Heritage Area contains over 1200 kilometres of roads, providing access to 200 recognised visitor sites. Some of these roads are narrow dirt tracks originally built for forestry logging.

Destinations in the Wet Tropics World Heritge Area

Northern Destinations	page
Captain Cook Highway – Oak Beach to Buchan Point	10
Mossman Gorge	11
Alexandra Range Lookout	13
Jindalba	14
Maardja Botanical Walk	15
Myall Beach-Dubuji	16
Cape Tribulation	17
Black Mountain	18

Tablelands Destinations	
Barron Falls	22
Bunda Bibandji (Bare Hill)	24
Lake Barrine	25
Lake Eacham	26
Cathedral Fig	27
Curtain Fig	28
Mount Bartle Frere	29
The Crater	30

Central Coast Destinations	
Crystal Cascades	34
Lake Morris	35
Walshs Pyramid	36
Babinda Boulders	37
Etty Bay	38
North Bramston Beach	39
Josephine Falls	40
Goldsborough Valley	41
Tchupala Falls	42
Nandroya Falls	43
Misty Mountains	44
Bicton Hill	45
Lacey Creek - Licuala	46

Noah Valley in Daintree National Park.

Northern Destinations

The coastal route north from Cairns is one of Australia's premier scenic drives. Along the Daintree coast, the largest remaining lowland rainforest in Australia tumbles down to meet fringing reef.

Above: Rex Lookout and Wangetti Beach.

Right: Looking north along Ellis Beach.

Captain Cook Highway
– Oak Beach to Buchan Point

The Captain Cook Highway closely hugs the coast along this section of the Macallister Range, making it one of the most picturesque driving routes in Australia. There is access to numerous beaches, however swimmers must be mindful of the box jellyfish season from November through to April.

The Rex Lookout provides a spectacular vista overlooking Wangetti Beach and the coastline to Palm Cove. The lookout is a popular location for launching hang gliders.

Above: Early morning cloud flows down the MacCalister Range.

Left: One of the many beaches along the Captain Cook Highway - Rex lookout visible on the distant headland.

Mossman Gorge

Crystal clear water flows through a river bed of large granite boulders surrounded by some of the most scenic lowland rainforest found in the region. Along a short, easy walk from the car park is a turquoise coloured pool where jungle perch and turtles are seen in abundance. A 2.7 km loop walk carries on up the gorge after crossing Rex Creek by a suspension bridge.

The Kuku Yalanji Dreamtime Tours conduct interpretive cultural walks through the national park and their adjoining land.

Above: Suspension foot-bridge over Rex Creek at Mossman Gorge.

Right: Crystal clear water of a pristine stream in the upper Mossman Gorge.

Left & above: The Mossman River is strewn with innumerable granite boulders, worn smooth from thousands of years of heavy rains.

Below: Golden Penda flowers festoon the trees along the river banks.

Alexandra Range Lookout

The lookout parking area was originally cleared and levelled as a potential house site. The land was purchased under the Daintree Rescue Program and added to Daintree National Park in the early 1990's.

The lookout provides a spectacular panoramic view of the Daintree River mouth, Low Isles, sections of the Great Barrier Reef and the Captain Cook Highway coastline as far south as Palm Cove.

Looking south from the Alexandra Range Lookout over the Daintree River mouth.

Jindalba

The Jindalba access road and carpark was a horse paddock purchased under the Daintree Rescue Program and rehabilitated. A 700m loop boardwalk provides interpretive signage, and a 2.7 km circuit track provides a more intimate rainforest experience for those with more time.

Adjoining the entrance to Jindalba is the Daintree Discovery Centre that features high quality interpretation, canopy walkways and tower.

A prominent feature of these sites is Angiopteris (or King Fern), the world's largest fern, with fronds up to six metres in length.

The aerial walkway at the Daintree Discovery Centre, next to Jindalba.

Maardja Botanical Walk

This 1km circuit pathway and boardwalk transects several forest types including lowland rainforest, seasonally inundated pandanus thickets and mangroves. Three-dimensional bronze cast displays along the boardwalk feature the various mangrove root structures.

 Situated in the Noah Valley, the walk is renowned for the many rare plants that are only found here. One such rarity is *Gardenia actinocarpa* that is only known to grow on the alluvial flats around the mouth of Noah Creek.

Above: Bronze mangrove root castings and interpretive signage along the Maardja boardwalk.

Right: Early morning light streams through light mist within the Oliver Creek mangroves.

Myall Beach–Dubuji

Myall Beach has direct access from the Cape Tribulation village through either the Dubuji day use area, or via a boardwalk through the mangroves along the northern boundary of Dubuji.

The Dubuji site features a 1.2 km loop boardwalk that traverses rainforest and "cut grass" swamp on the dunes and swales behind the beach.

A walking track leads from the northern end of Myall Beach, over the headland into the Cape Tribulation day use area and beach. Access to this track from the beach may be blocked at high tide.

Left: Aerial view looking south over Myall Beach and Mason Creek.

Above: Fringing reef exposed at low tide on Myall Beach with Cape Tribulation Headland.

Cape Tribulation

Lieutenant James Cook named the Cape "Tribulation" when his ship *Endeavour* struck the nearby Great Barrier Reef in 1770.

"Cape Trib" was made famous in 1983 as the site where protestors demonstrated against the State Government's controversial construction of the Bloomfield Road/Track. The now completed route links Cape Tribulation with the Wujal Wujal community and provides a coastal route to Cooktown.

It is now better known as the place where the rainforest meets the reef, or by it's Aboriginal name - Kulki. A 400m pathway and boardwalk leads to a viewing platform that provides an excellent vista of Mount Sorrow summit, the fringing reef off Cape Trib beach and the coast north to the mouth of Emmagen Creek.

Above: Coconut Beach.

Right: View looking south from the Bloomfield Track of Cape Tribulation.

Black Mountain

The main road to Cooktown passes through a gap in the northern end of the Black Trevethan Range providing spectacular views of this massive pyramid-shaped pile of granite boulders. The black colouration is caused by a layer of algae growing over the exposed rock surface.

The mountain is honeycombed with caves that are home to several animal species found nowhere else. Access is extremely difficult and treacherous. Over the years there have been several reports of people vanishing, having fallen between the rocks never to be found.

Left: The Cooktown Road is just visible as it winds through the boulder massifs of the Black Trevethan Range.

View looking west from Mount Bellenden Ker to the Atherton Tablelands.

Tablelands Destinations

The Tablelands has a relaxed, rural atmosphere and offers visitors easy access to extinct volcanic lakes, waterfalls and cool, scenic rainforest drives as well as many options for food and accomodation. This makes the Tablelands a popular destination for locals and visitors of all ages.

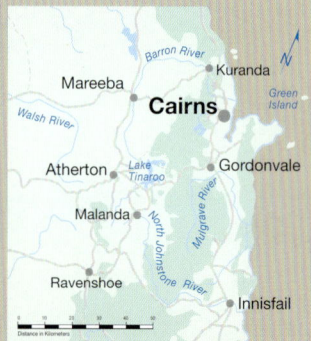

Above: The Kuranda Scenic Railway's locomotives are decorated illustrating Djabugay lore.

Barron Falls

The headwaters of the Barron River are on the Atherton Tableland. Two-thirds of the area was cleared of rainforest as the rich red-brown volcanic soil was prized for farming. As a consequence, the Barron Falls now flows red whenever in flood.

The Kuranda Scenic Railway traverses the southern side of the Barron Gorge, with viewing decks at the Barron Falls Station providing the best vantage point to view the falls. Visitors can gain road access to the Barron Falls Station from Kuranda. The walking track from the car park to the station incorporates a rainforest canopy walk 14 metres above a creek. The Barron Falls Station is the most visited site within the WTWHA.

The Skyrail Cableway traverses the northern side of the gorge, providing excellent views from the gondolas as well as viewing decks and a rainforest interpretation centre.

Far Left: Barron River in flood at the Barron Hydro Power station.

Left: View from the Barron Falls Railway Station of the Barron Falls in flood.

Above: Canopy walkway on route to the Barron Falls Railway Station and viewing area.

Right: Skyrail Cableway provides visitors with unique views of the rainforest.

Bunda Dibandji (Bare Hill)

Historically this area was a powerful place for the resident Buluwandji Tribe, speakers of the Djabugandji language for whom certain locations held specific meanings and functions.

The rock art sites where boardwalks have been installed are traditional public sites that tell cultural stories. Some places were used for men's initiations, while others were sites for women only. For this reason, visitors may access the site only in the company of a guide who has been endorsed by the tribal elders.

The ridge where Bare Hill is situated is the western extremity of the rainforest and the WTWHA boundary. A 700m walking track climbs to the rock art site.

The large cycads growing near the walking track still retain foothold scars that were cut out with stone axes to enable climbing to harvest their seeds.

Above: viewing area at a rock art site.

Left: View of Bare Hill mid way along the walking track to the art sites.

Lake Barrine

Lake Barrine was formed during a period of active volcanism about 12,000 years ago. It is thought that the underground water table became super heated, resulting in an enormous explosion leaving this deep crater. A small creek drains off the overflow, keeping the lake at a fairly constant 65m depth at its centre.

A 6.5 km walking track circles the lake.

The twin kauri trees at the track entrance are believed to be about 1,100 years old. Much of the farmland of the Atherton Tableland once contained giants such as these.

Above: These giant twin kauris are found near the start of the walking track.

Right: The water level at Lake Barrine remains constant all year round.

Lake Eacham

Formed in the same way and at the same time as Lake Barrine, Eacham maintains a crater rim that prevents water run off either into or out of the lake.

As the lake remained isolated from all other water bodies since its creation, it developed as a unique ecosystem. The ease of access to the lake enabled people to introduce a range of aquatic species that have decimated the indigenous species and altered the ecosystem.

During the past 12,000 years, wind-blown pollen grains fell onto the lake's surface, settling in fine layers onto the lakebed. These layers of silt and preserved pollen tell the history of cyclic changes in vegetation growth within the crater. Over this period, changing climate favoured rainforest some of the time and eucalypt forest at other times.

A 4.5 km walking track circles the lake.

Above: Pandanus grow in dense thickets along the lake's shore.

Cathedral Fig

This magnificent specimen of a strangler fig (*Ficus virens*) clearly illustrates this species' survival strategy. Originally, its tiny seeds would have been deposited in the droppings of flying foxes or birds in the canopy of a tree. The seedling focused its energies in developing a root system. When the roots reached the nutrient-rich leaf litter on the ground the branches began to grow, high up in the canopy where there was an abundance of light.

As the fig grew, it produced more and more roots. Over many years they merged together forming a constricting network that stopped the growth of its host tree and ultimately caused its death.

Curtain Fig

This is the same species as the Cathedral Fig. The difference here is that when the fig was very small, it's host tree fell over against another tree and rested there at about a 60 degree angle. Parts of the dead host tree are still visible.

As its root growth is influenced by gravity, these just kept growing downwards like streamers until they hit the ground. The result after an estimated 500 years of growth is a "curtain-like" effect standing 40m tall with a circumference of 39m.

Mount Bartle Frere

At an altitude of 1622m, Mount Bartle Frere is Queensland's highest peak. A steep 8.1 km walking track commences at Josephine Falls, while a 7 km walking track commences at the end of the Gourka Road on the Atherton Tableland.

Bush campsites are available near the summit. At this altitude the weather is highly variable, fine and sunny one moment, foggy and freezing the next.

When not covered in cloud, the summit affords spectacular views of the coastal plain and the entire Atherton Tablelands.

Above & Right: The walking track to the summit passes through granite boulder fields. Ferns and shrubs grow in the open patches on the mountain top.

The Crater

This volcanic pipe is believed to have been formed by the explosion of subterranean gases. The pipe is 70m in diameter and extends to a depth of 140m below the crater's rim, before veering off horizontally for an unknown distance.

This area is the headwaters of the Barron River. This river flows though farmland on the Atherton Tableland to reach Lake Tinaroo, then drops over the falls at Kuranda to its mouth near the Cairns airport.

The Crater is a popular, all weather site for spotlighting nocturnal wildlife such as Herbert River ringtail possums, Lumholtz tree kangaroos, leaf-tailed geckos, frogs etc.

Left: A viewing platform extends out beyond the rim of the crater providing a clear view to the bottom.

Tully River at the Recreation Park campground.

Central Coast Destinations

Central Coast Destinations

The Bruce Highway meanders past mill towns, cane fields and fruit farms along the Central Coast from Cairns to Cardwell. To the east lie isolated tropical beaches. To the west loom rugged mountains laced with rainforest, waterfalls and walks. If you're lucky, you may see an endangered cassowary...

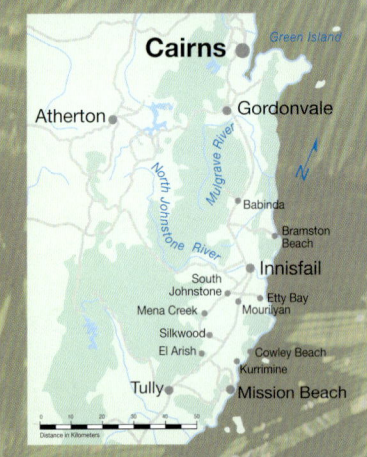

Right: Fan Palm Licuala ramsyi.

Crystal Cascades

Access was originally constructed for the Cairns water supply. This scenic, narrow gorge with its numerous cascades and pools becomes a popular swimming location during the summer months.

A 1.2 km pathway hugs the side of Freshwater Creek, with numerous access points to swimming holes in the lower section. Be aware of the stinging trees, which commonly grow along the edge of the walking track.

Above: Stinging tree in fruit.

Left: One of the many pools popular with swimmers at Crystal Cascades.

Lake Morris
Copperlode Dam

The building of a dam for the Cairns water supply at Copperlode Falls created this "lake in the rainforest". Crystal Cascades is situated immediately downstream, while Lambs Head looms above the lake.

Commercial 4x4 tours cross over the dam wall to traverse the Clohesy River Road. Recreation is not permitted on the lake, however a kiosk and picnic area are situated at a vantage point above the dam, providing a panoramic vista.

Lake Morris at Copperlode Dam.

Walshs Pyramid

A rough, steep walking track leads to the summit at 900 metres elevation. Being solid granite, only a sparse eucalypt forest with grassy understorey survives where soil accumulates. Resurrection plants grow on the exposed rock slopes. These normally vibrant green herbs dry to a bright orange colour, then turn green again with rain as if resurrected.

An annual footrace to the summit and back is held as part of the Gordonvale Fair in August.

In Aboriginal lore, this rock formation is a large turkey's mound.

Left: Walsh's Pyramid looms above the Mulgrave River.

Above: Resurrection plants turn a burnt orange colour during the dry season

Babinda Boulders

Granite boulders, crystal clear waters and deep swimming holes within pristine rainforest make for a popular site.

This is the trailhead for the 19 km Goldfields Trail to Kearneys Flat within the Goldsborough Valley. The trail derives its name from the gold mines established in the 1930's that are situated on Coronation Hill, above the causeway half way along this trail.

Above: Swift floodwaters have sculptured and polished these granite boulders.

Right: Granite boulders and crystal clear water.

Etty Bay

This beautiful beach, surrounded by rainforest of the Moresby Range National Park, is one of the few remaining locations where cassowaries can be readily seen. They may be seen walking along the beach.

Left: Metamorphic rocks at the southern end of Etty Bay.

Top: Large Callophylum trees grow right up to the high tide line.

Above: A solitary coconut rises above the beach rainforest.

North Bramston Beach

A small, picturesque campground is provided at the northern end of Bramston Beach. Wyvuri Swamp, known for its pitcher (insectivorous) plants, drains into an estuary that marks the southern limit of Graham Range.

Large estuarine crocodiles are known to exist here. Do not swim or wash in this creek.

Top: Leached tannins from Wyvuri Swamp gives the water a coffee colour leaving tide lines along the sand.

Right: Bramston Beach

Josephine Falls

Situated within dense rainforest, it is impossible to see the build up of heavy cloud and rain on the summit of Mount Bartle Frere immediately above. Within minutes, a flash flood can rise several metres in height, stranding or washing away unwary swimmers. Many have drowned in the treacherous plunge pool below the top falls, and more have sustained serious injuries from slipping while attempting to cross the smooth rock.

An 8.1 km walking track leads to the summit of Mount Bartle Frere, and a 600m pathway leads to Josephine Falls viewing platforms.

Left: This bottom pool is the only swimming hole. Access to Josephine Falls upstream is only permitted via the boardwalks and viewing platforms.

Goldsborough Valley

Situated on the Mulgrave River beneath Mount Bellenden Ker, Kearneys Flat is a popular spot for swimming and camping.

A short walk leads to Kearneys Falls. The campground is also the trailhead for the 19 km Goldfields Trail emerging at Babinda Boulders.

Kearneys Flat was historically a dry season camp for the Malanburra clan of the Yidinydjii Aboriginal tribe. Before the onset of the wet season, these people would walk to the tablelands around the Gadgarra area, moving back to the valley for the following dry season.

The present day campground was built on the site of an Aboriginal burial ground.

Above: Gnarled and disfigured water gums survive the annual wet season floods.

Right: The Mulgrave River has numerous pools suitable for swimming.

Tchupala Falls

The waterfall is a short 600m from the parking area on the Palmerston Highway.

Another track branches off to reach Wallicher Falls at 900m and follows Henrietta Creek for 2 km to reach Goolagan Picnic Area with a further 800m to Henrietta Creek Campground and the start of Nandroya Falls circuit track.

Left: Tchupala consists of numerous flows gauging through the chocolate brown lava rock.

Above: The fruits of Pothos longipes is abundant and was a staple food for the MaMu people.

Nandroya Falls

A 7.5 km circuit walking track commences at Henrietta Creek campground on the Palmerston Highway. Of the many waterfalls in the region, Nandroya is one of the most scenic.

In 1882, Christie Palmerston, accompanied by Aboriginal guides, explored the area following Aboriginal pathways that connected their camps. The present alignment of the Palmerston Highway now follows this route. An Aboriginal bora ground (a circular clearing within the rainforest where ceremonies were conducted) can be seen on the side of the highway near the Ranger's Station at Crawfords Lookout.

Nandroya consists of a narrow, upper fall and a broad, lower fall.

Misty Mountains

The Misty Mountains Trail network consists of 130 km of walking tracks and roads though upland rainforest. The tracks vary in length from the trip to Bally's Knob suitable for a day walk (12km return) while others are long-distance overnight camping expeditions such as Koolmoon Creek track (35.5km one way).

These tracks traverse rugged, remote country. Any person intending to walk any sections should contact the nearest National Parks information centre to seek up to date information about the road access, maps, track conditions, water availability and campsite bookings.

One of the highlights along the Misty Mountains Trail is the tall, cascading Elizabeth Grant Falls.

Bicton Hill

A 2 km walking track commencing at Bingil Bay terminates at Bicton Hill within Clump Mountain National Park. The summit lookout provides views of Dunk Island, Family Group of Islands, Mission Beach coast and the towering mountains of Hinchinbrook Island. Cassowaries may sometimes be encountered along this track.

View from the summit lookout at Bicton Hill showing Dunk Island.

Lacey Creek - Licuala

Lacey Creek has a 1.1 km loop walk through coastal lowland rainforest. Situated along the walk is a cassowary interpretive shelter and an arboretum.

Licuala has a 1.2 km loop walk through abundant stands of Licuala fan palms. These spectacular fan palms are only found within the wet tropics rainforests.

A 7 km walking track connects these two sites. Visitors have a very good chance of seeing cassowaries in their natural habitat at these locations.

Cassowaries can suddenly emerge from the rainforest to cross the roads. Speeding motorists have killed many birds. Please drive slowly in known cassowary habitats.

Above: Licuala palms are the dominant plants of this area.

Below: Cassowaries can step out onto the road at any time during the day.

Right: Picnickers are fenced in to prevent cassowaries stealing food.

46

Wallaman Falls plunges over the sheer wall of Stony Creek Gorge.

Southern Destinations

Southern Destinations

Waterfalls, rivers and mosaics of rainforest and open forest captivate visitors to the Southern Wet Tropics. Don't miss Australia's highest single drop waterfall, the 305m Wallaman Falls. It's a spectacular starting point for the 110km Wet Tropics Great Walk to Blencoe Falls…

Rafting is a popular activity on the Tully River.

Tully River

A 380m circuit track through rainforest provides informative signage about the large gatherings of butterflies that are commonly seen between September and February.

At the head of Tully Gorge is Tully Falls, once one of the largest waterfalls in Australia. Koombooloomba Dam was built upstream, diverting the Tully River from the falls through a tunnel to drive the Kareeya Hydro Power Station. The Tully Falls now flow only when Koombooloomba Dam overflows during cyclonic events.

Commercial rafting is conducted daily on the white water rapids of the Tully River. The rafts enter the river adjacent to the Kareeya Hydro Power Station at the road terminus and exit at the campground downstream. The river flattens out at this point making it suitable for swimming.

Far left: One of the many streams plunging into the Tully River.

Left: The upper reaches of the Tully River consists of rough white water rapids.

Above: The lower reaches of the Tully River consists of flat water.

Murray Falls

This popular camping and swimming destination has a sinister reputation for taking life. Many people have fallen over the waterfall, or drowned in these swift flowing waters.

There is a viewing platform at the base of the falls. A 900m walking track leads to a viewing platform at the top of the falls that provides panoramic views of the upper Murray Valley. Walking anywhere near the waterfall is now prohibited.

The only access around the Murray Falls is via boardwalks and viewing platforms.

Jourama Falls

Lower rainfall is the primary reason for the dominance of open eucalypt forest at Jourama. A 1.5 km walking track climbs from the camp ground to Jourama Falls Lookout. The water flow can be very low at the end of the dry season. Heavy rain will flood Jourama Creek, blocking road and walking track access.

Left: Jourama consists of a series of falls plunging down this exposed escarpment.

Above: Eucalypts with grassy ground cover characterise the drier open ridges.

Wet Tropics Great Walk

This network of walking trails and cross country hiking feature the open forest escarpment country of the Herbert River Gorge. Three main entry/exit points provide access to a range of day and overnight walks including:

Buujan Quiinbira walk – 37.5 km one way from Wallaman Falls to Yamanie Section pickup;

Jaygany (goanna) walk – 57 km one way from Wallaman Falls to Henrietta gate; and

Gugigugi (butterfly) walk – 38 km one way from Henrietta gate to Yamanie Section pickup;

Yamanie pick up to Orange tree – 7 km one way;

Juwun walk - 10.5 km 0ne way from Blencoe Falls to Blanket Creek ; and

For the very adventurous, a cross country trek along the Hertbert River Gorge from Blencoe Falls to exiting at either Yamanie Section pickup, Henrietta gate or Wallaman Falls.

These tracks traverse rugged, remote country. Any person intending to walk any sections should contact the nearest National Parks information centre.

Previous page: The spectacular Blencoe Falls with Hoop Pine forest in the gorge.

Above and right: The Wet Tropics Great Walk is a trail that traverses the rim of the Herbert Gorge.

Broadwater

A picturesque campground is situated on the river flat of Broadwater Creek, surrounded by a mix of eucalypt forest and rainforest. A 3 km walking track follows Broadwater Creek upstream to the clear water pools of the "Overflow". Multicoloured river stones, including pink granite, white quartz and black basalt, are visible through the crystal clear waters.

A 1.6 km rainforest circuit track features a 50m high fig tree with massive buttresses.

Above: Broadwater Creek contains an array of multicoloured stones.

Right: Clear, shallow pools – ideal for cooling off

Wallaman Falls

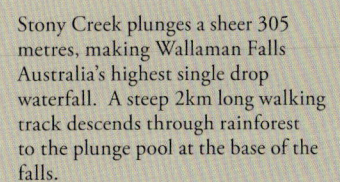

Stony Creek plunges a sheer 305 metres, making Wallaman Falls Australia's highest single drop waterfall. A steep 2km long walking track descends through rainforest to the plunge pool at the base of the falls.

Platypus are often seen in Stony Creek upstream from the falls. It is amazing to imagine that platypus had in the past scaled Wallaman Falls, or had traversed cross country to access the upper reaches of Stony Creek. In reality, platypus have existed in the area in excess of 100 million years, so they were probably living in the creek before the falls were formed.

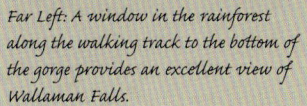

Far Left: A window in the rainforest along the walking track to the bottom of the gorge provides an excellent view of Wallaman Falls.

Left: Platypus can be seen swimming in Stony Creek near the campground.

Paluma

The drive up the Paluma Range provides impressive views of deeply carved creek valleys and changing vegetation types. Rainforest gullies give way to drier ridges dominated by hoop pine, eucalypts and turpentine trees.

Little Crystal Creek, 7 km up the range, provides a cool dip during the summer heat. Views of the coastal plain (provided the fog is not in), including Palm and Orpheus Islands, can be enjoyed from McClellands Lookout on the edge of the escarpment at Paluma village.

Far left: Little Crystal Creek is fringed with majestic hoop pines.

Left: Little Crystal Creek, below the stone arch bridge, provides cool water holes.

Right: Paluma Range is a mix of vegetation types.